DAILY HERALD

No. 12938 (C) Saturday October 5, 1957 PRICE 2d.

First earth satellite goes round the world in 95 minutes

RUSSIA WINS RACE INTO OUTER SPACE

A SATELLITE is today circling the earth at a height of 560 miles. It is the first earth satellite ever launched. And it is Russia's.

It was launched yesterday, according to an announcement by Tass, the Soviet News Agency.

TRACK BY RADAR

"It is at present describing an elliptical trajectory around the earth," said the message.

It is in the form of a sphere, it added, and carries a radar transmitter. It is about the size of a medicine ball—23 inches across—and weighs 180lb.

Less than three weeks ago the Russians declared that a satellite would be launched soon. The angle at which it was to be fired made it clear that it should pass over Britain.

Radar will be able to track its path.

It will be possible to watch its flight in the rays of the setting or rising sun, says Tass, with the aid of ordinary binoculars.

Tass says the launching was from a carrier rocket which gave the satellite a speed of about 26,000ft. a second—or 18,000 miles an hour.

It can therefore encircle the earth in an hour and 35 minutes—no longer than one of today's football matches will last.

Moscow has been told that it will be seen twice over the city today—at 1.46 a.m. and at 6.42 a.m., Moscow time.

Amateur radio operators will be able to pick up the signals which the satellite is transmitting continuously, says Tass.

MR. K SAID—

The claim means that Russia has beaten the Western world in the race to conquer space.

Two-and-a-half years ago America officially announced that the construction and launching of small unmanned satellites had been approved by the U.S. Government for America's part in the International Geophysical Year researches.

It was immediately followed by an announcement from Russia—Mr. Kruschev himself made it—that the U S S R would support the idea and also launch satellites of their own.

A Soviet scientist, Professor A. A. Blaonravov, told a meeting in Washington last night that Russia's satellites would stay aloft up to 15 months in an orbit of up to 500 miles, or 30 years in an orbit of up to 935 miles.

Calculations are believed to show that owing to its tremendous speed the satellite would burn up on reaching denser layers of the atmosphere at the end of its existence.

Later last night Tass said that Russia proposed launching several more artificial satellites, bigger than yesterday's.

'FRIENDLY'

In **New York**, television commentators said that the Soviet claim, if true, meant the Russians had won what had been described as a friendly contest with the United States in the International Geophysical Year.

The United States plans to launch its first man-made satellite early next spring.

Experts believe that Russia's contribution to the International Geophysical Year — recently launched on BBC TV by the Duke of Edinburgh—has been accelerated by the assistance of German scientists who helped to produce the rockets which bombarded Britain towards the end of the war.

Britain's contribution to this important upper atmosphere research during the International Geophysical Year has been limited economically. And the battle has been between America and Russia.

The Russian effort must have cost them little less than £4million to achieve.

Last night, however, scientists throughout the world were wondering why Russia had not advertised the first flight of their satellite beforehand. One of the most important facets of this research work is that to gain any benefit the progress of the satellite must be charted by observers, using electronic devices, in every corner of the earth.

COSMIC RAYS

This Russian satellite is exactly similar in proportion to the American type and packed tight with instruments which can record such things as the effects of cosmic rays. Does all this mean that we are on the verge of space travel?

No. To send a satellite which could carry a man the same distance as this "football" would cost many hundreds of millions of pounds.

And it must be remembered that these tiny unmanned "footballs" will circle the earth at heights only a fraction of that of the distance we should need to travel to reach the moon.

● *An artist's version of the satellite and how it circles the earth*

OFF IT!

WHAT is Mr. Iain Macleod trying to do? Wheedle or bully, or do both at once?

He raises the cry of "intimidation" and "political blackmail" against "leaders of the Labour Party."

Why? Because the Government can't get its own way with the trade unions. Because the trade unions will not lie down to be trampled on and say: "Yes, sir, three bags full," to policies like the Rent Act.

This is worse than political claptrap from the Minister of Labour. It is political war-mongering.

Free-for-all

The Government has done nothing to gain the goodwill of the trade unions. It has forced a free-for-all upon the country and forced the trade unions to join in to protect their members. **BUT IT STILL HANKERS TO IMPOSE ONE-SIDED RESTRAINT.**

"The future course of unemployment," says Mr. Macleod, "depends on the wisdom of those who claim *or concede* wage demands. . . ."

"No-one welcomes strikes, but we must not be afraid of them. . . ."

"It is no part of my job to seek peace at any price."

Who is trying to blackmail whom?

Mr. Macleod's is an important and ominous speech. Perhaps a fatal speech.

We can tell Mr. Macleod one thing. This is not the way that any Minister of Labour should speak to the trade unions.

'Mrs. THOMPSON' CITED WITH DUKE'S FRIEND

MRS. EILEEN PARKER
"I can say nothing about Mrs. Thompson."

Parker's wife sues him for divorce

MRS. EILEEN PARKER, wife of 36-year-old Commander Michael Parker, former Private Secretary to the Duke of Edinburgh, filed petition for divorce yesterday.

Mrs. Parker, who is 34, alleges adultery by her husband with a Mrs. Mary Thompson.

At her flat in Launceston-place, Kensington, last night, Mrs. Eileen Parker said: "I can say absolutely nothing about Mrs. Thompson. I do not know where she is."

Was Mrs. Thompson in this country at the moment? "I cannot answer that, either," said Mrs. Parker. "I don't know. I must refer all these questions to my solicitor."

22 days

When would the hearing take place? "It may be weeks or months before the petition is heard," she said. "That, too, is a matter for my solicitor."

And she closed the door.

Lieut.-Commander Parker has 22 days in which to file a defence to the suit, if he wishes. The same applies to Mrs. Thompson.

It was in February—only 48 hours after Scots-born wife Eileen revealed that she and her husband had parted—that Lieut-Commander Parker resigned as the Duke's Private Secretary.

Friends said at the time that there was a chance of a reconciliation. They were wrong.

And in Melbourne, Parker's father, Captain Charles Parker, attributed the breakdown of the marriage to his son's absence on royal visits abroad.

Parker first met the Duke in 1941 at Scapa Flow, when they were both destroyer officers.

A Wren

Two years later, while commissioning a minesweeper in Scotland, the Lt.-Commander met the girl who was to become his wife, Wren Eileen Allan, of Troon, Ayrshire.

Parker's friendship with the Duke continued. In 1952, the Duke made him Private Secretary, at a salary believed to be about £1,500 a year.

The Parkers have two children, Michael, 11, and Julie, eight. The Duke is Julie's godfather.

Wilson tells of leak evidence

By TREVOR WILLIAMS

A SENSATIONAL declaration that he has *prima facie* evidence of a leak "from a political source" before the Bank Rate went up to seven per cent., was made by Mr. Harold Wilson, Labour's Shadow Chancellor, yesterday.

He made it to Mr. Enoch Powell, Financial Secretary to the Treasury, in a letter, repeating Labour's demand for a public inquiry.

But last night the Prime Minister, Mr. Macmillan, wrote back to Mr. Wilson rejecting the demand.

However, his letter ended: "If you are willing to make it *(the evidence)* available to me, I am prepared to refer it to the Lord Chancellor, and ask him whether it affords sufficient ground for further investigation."

It has been said that as a result of leakage, Stock Exchange deals involving £4million to £10million—according to varying estimates—took place between the evening of September 18 and the morning of September 19.

The new rate was announced at midday on the 19th.

Suspicion

Mr. Wilson said in his letter that not only did he have the evidence, but he was ready to make it available to any inquiry the Government cared to set up.

The Government's refusal to order an inquiry "cannot be left where it is," he wrote.

"Both in the Press and the City there is widespread concern and more than a suspicion that an improper leakage took place, and that the Government has something to hide.

"On far less circumstantial evidence Lord Attlee, as Prime Minister, ordered a full public inquiry when similar suggestions were made."

The letter goes on: "You have apparently briefly consulted the Governor of the Bank of England, the Government broker and the chairman of the Stock Exchange.

"The first is the head of a department which must be involved in any inquiries . . . and the Government broker is under criticism in the City for pushing gilt-edged immediately before the change.

"The chairman of the Stock Exchange would be the first to agree that his members are not involved, except as sufferers from any leak that may have taken place."

The letter concludes: "It is really no answer to say that only £4million worth of gilt-edged changed hands on the afternoon and evening of September 18.

"The committee appointed following Mr. Hugh Dalton's resignation found that no money changed hands."

YOU AND YOUR MONEY...

'CUT cost of living'

TORY failure to bring down the cost of living was condemned at the Labour Party conference yesterday.

A resolution debated at Brighton urged the stabilisation of prices, pegging of profits, and removal of purchase tax on necessities.

Morgan Phillips, the Party Secretary, said that food prices had risen by 45 per cent. under the Tory Government and the £ had dropped to 15s. 9d. in value.

The resolution was remitted to the Executive and a Working Party for a report at next year's conference.

(Conference Report—Page Two)

UP goes mortgage

MILLIONS of people who are buying their homes on mortgages may soon have to pay more.

One small building society, the Lion, yesterday raised its rates to borrowers from 6½ per cent. to 7.

So a man who has borrowed £2,000 on his house will have to pay 12s. 1d. a month more in repayment.

Big societies — among them Co-op —are Soci Lion Th Octo its r go u

---

Night of fear as Warsaw workers riot

AMBULANCES with sirens screaming were still gathering up the injured early today after steel-helmeted Warsaw militiamen, armed with revolvers, and swinging rubber-truncheons, charged 20,000 "freedom" demonstrators in the city square.

Wave after wave of shouting men was swept back. Their banner, saying in foot-high letters "Away with the Gestapo . . . Freedom for the Press," crashed down and was torn to shreds.

But the crowd rallied. The outnumbered militiamen, joined by police, began throwing tear-gas bombs.

The demonstrators, screaming "Po Prostu," retaliated. They ripped up paving-stones and hurled them at the militiamen.

"Po Prostu" is a students' newspaper that has just been banned. Thousands of students who protested against the censorship on Thursday were beaten up.

But the outbreak last night was even more violent as workers, backing the students, tried to march on the Communist Party H Q.

UNCONSCIOUS

Lorry loads of regular troops stood by in reserve with machine guns as the militiamen battled with the crowd.

One man of about 60 screamed out "Fascists" . . . and was immediately clubbed by two militiamen.

A man shouted: "Swine," and jumped on a moving tram . . . in vain.

A squad of militiamen stopped the vehicle. Three climbed on and dragged the frightened demonstrator from his seat.

They beat him unconscious and left him on the pavement.

Women were dragged away by their hair. A boy of 15 who booed the militia was clubbed senseless.

For the first time there were shouts of, "Down with Gomulka."

SURROUNDED

Wladyslaw Gomulka is the Communist leader who "de-Stalinised" the Polish regime.

Yet it was *Po Prostu* that swept Gomulka to power.

That's why the crowd, swept away from the polytechnic, chanted "Traitor" and tried to march on the Communist Party headquarters.

They never reached the seven-storey building. Hundreds of militiamen had cordoned off the streets and the H Q itself was surrounded by Regular troops.

Trucks raced militia reinforcements to the scene and the demonstrators didn't have a chance.

They were bludgeoned to a standstill, then forced back.

Clocks back tomorrow

Summer Time ends at 2 a.m. tomorrow. Clocks should be put back an hour.

...ny triplet dies

...y boy of the triplets ...ellingborough (North-...Wednesday to 20-year-...ne Brayford, British-... of an American ex-...n, died yesterday.

WHEN I WAS YOUNG
THE FIFTIES

NEIL THOMSON
MEETS
PAT SCOTT (NÉE HOWE)

FRANKLIN WATTS
LONDON   NEW YORK   SYDNEY   TORONTO

Pat Scott was born in North London in 1946, a year after the end of the Second World War. There was a shortage of accommodation in London and the family lived in cramped conditions.

In 1953, when she was seven, Pat's family moved from London to Harlow New Town in Essex.

Pat went to local schools in Harlow and saw the town expand during the 1950s. She went to teacher training college and now teaches maths in a Harlow secondary school.

Pat is married with two children and lives with her family in Harlow, near to where she teaches.

Copyright © 1991 Franklin Watts

First published in Great Britain by
Franklin Watts
96 Leonard Street
London
EC2A 4RH

Franklin Watts Australia
14 Mars Road
Lane Cove
N.S.W. 2066

ISBN: 0 7496 0527 8

CONTENTS

Family life in London

My name is Pat Scott. I was born in London in 1946. My brother Geoff was born four years later. We lived with our parents in Tottenham in North London. My dad had been a Japanese prisoner of war. When he came home in 1945 he married my mum. They had lived in the same street when they were kids.

It was difficult to find housing after the war so we shared a house with another family. We didn't have much space, with only two rooms for the four of us. There was no bathroom in our house and only an outside toilet in the garden. We used old newspaper instead of toilet roll.

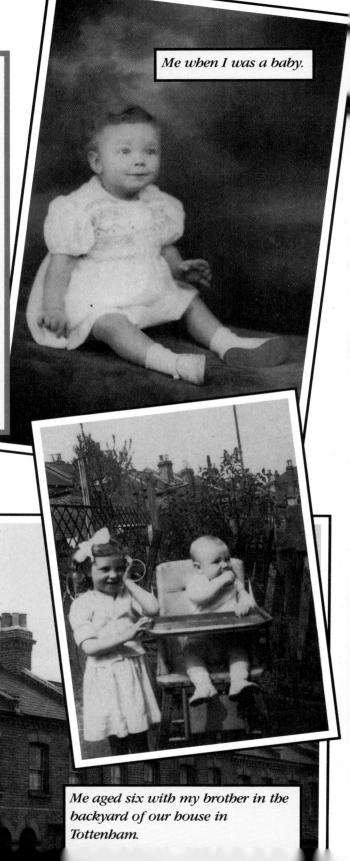

Me when I was a baby.

Minster Road, where Pat lived, is no longer there. The area has been redeveloped. Many buildings in London were damaged by German bombs during the war.

Me aged six with my brother in the backyard of our house in Tottenham.

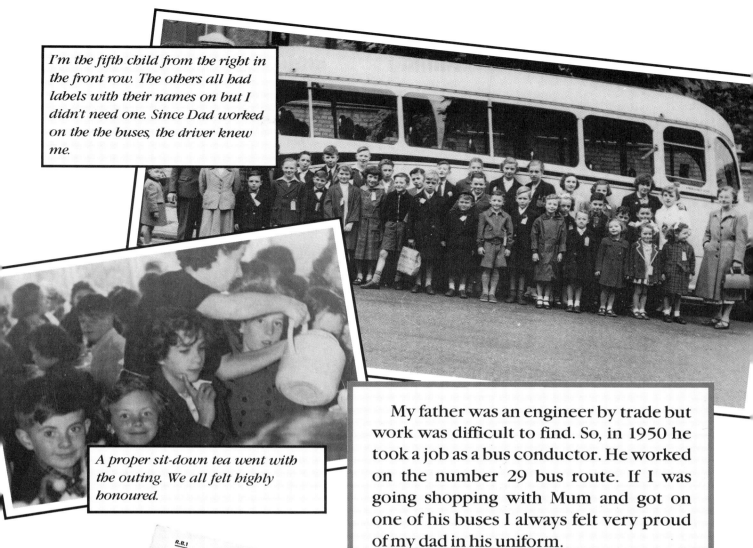

I'm the fifth child from the right in the front row. The others all had labels with their names on but I didn't need one. Since Dad worked on the the buses, the driver knew me.

A proper sit-down tea went with the outing. We all felt highly honoured.

MINISTRY OF FOOD
1953-1954
SERIAL NO. 1
BQ 366830
RATION BOOK
Surname

6 ENTER NAMES AND ADDRESSES OF RETAILERS

Food shortages carried on for several years after the end of the Second World War. The government continued to issue ration books to each household. Shopkeepers had to tear out a coupon for each sale of food in short supply.

My father was an engineer by trade but work was difficult to find. So, in 1950 he took a job as a bus conductor. He worked on the number 29 bus route. If I was going shopping with Mum and got on one of his buses I always felt very proud of my dad in his uniform.

The highlight of the year was the annual works outing for children. I don't remember where we went. The best thing was the sit-down tea, with more food than you could eat. That didn't happen very often at home as food was a bit scarce.

Mum didn't work when I was little. She was kept pretty busy looking after Geoff and me. We had lots of relatives nearby and we spent most of our time playing in the street and round their houses. We were allowed to go around the block by ourselves but not any further.

The Coronation

Queen Elizabeth's coronation in 1953 was a great event in our street. Several days beforehand the houses were decorated with flags. On Coronation Day there was a big party in the street with lots of tables all laid out with masses of sandwiches and ice cream. The mums and dads sat indoors watching the ceremony on television and the kids played outside.

We hired a television specially for the Coronation and then kept it on afterwards. It was very small and had a really curved screen to try and make the picture look bigger. Everything was in black and white then. I didn't watch much, only children's programmes like *Muffin the Mule*.

I dressed up in my pretend nurse's uniform on Coronation Day. It was the only special outfit that Mum could afford.

25 million people in Britain watched the Coronation on television. These army personnel in West Berlin gathered together to watch the big event.

Solitary In The Shining Radiance Of Her Young Beauty

QUEEN ELIZABETH II IS CROWNED

Ring CENtral 6000

WEATHER FORECAST
UNTIL NOON TO-MORROW:
Fresh, squally, northerly winds; showers, mostly this afternoon, when they may be heavy at times with hail and thunder in places; showers dying out in time tonight, evening rather fine. Showers too little external change, but the rather rough.
CHANNEL: rather steady.
BAROMETER: 29.65in. falling.
Lighting-up time 10.23 p.m. Sun sets 8.4 p.m. rises 4.47 a.m. Moon sets 9.58 p.m.; rises 12.43 a.m. To-morrow: Sun sets 8.5 p.m., rises 4.46 a.m. High water to-morrow, last quarter next Thursday, last quarter, London Bridge 5.48 a.m., 5.54 p.m.

The Evening News proudly presents
PAGE TWO: John Connell's description of The Crowning Moment. Gwen Robyns' impressions of the Abbey scene from the women's point of view.
PAGE THREE: James A. Jones' pen-picture of the gaiety, the colour along the processional route.
PAGE SIX: The conquest of Everest.

Westminster Abbey.

IN that ancient Abbey of Westminster to-day Elizabeth the Second was crowned Queen.

And from the Royal box a small boy, in white shirt and knickers watched, his hands clasping the gallery ledge, solemn eyes peeping over the top.

He saw his mother, the Crown upon her head, seated on her golden throne. And he saw his father, the Duke of Edinburgh, touch the Queen's head and kiss her gently upon the left cheek.

And there, momentarily, the Queen touched her right eye with her hand.

AT home, in Buckingham Palace, Princess Anne waited. She had waved good-bye as the Queen and the Duke drove away through the hundreds of thousands who were there to-day to cry their loyalty and their love.

She waited while Elizabeth of England was Crowned, while the guns boomed and the bells tolled and the Queen came from the Abbey to her people.

THE QUEEN LEAVES

The Queen left Coronation theatre at 1.35 p.m.

SIR W. STRANG ILL IN ABBEY

Sir William Strang, Permanent Under-Secretary for Foreign Affairs, and senior representative of Foreign Office at Coronation, collapsed in a faint during Abbey service to-day. Condition not serious.

1953 THE CORONATION

DIEU ET MON DROIT   HONI SOIT QUI MAL Y PENSE

Royal Pageant

Radiant in her Coronation robes—a close-up of the Queen in her State coach on her way to the Abbey.

The solemn moment approaches. Seated in her chair ... about to take the Oath, the Queen in dialogue with the Archbishop of Canterbury, makes solemn promises to govern with justice and mercy.

7

Family life in Harlow

Times were hard for us in London. Dad felt he wasn't getting anywhere as a bus conductor and Mum was fed up with living in a couple of rooms. A lot of people around us were looking for somewhere better to live. Dad heard about Harlow New Town from a friend who'd moved out there. Harlow was popular with people from North London since it wasn't too far to go. One Monday Dad took the day off work and went to have a look.

Dad found an engineering job advertised in the Harlow paper. He applied for it and a week later he heard he'd got the job.

It was easy then to find a house in Harlow if you had a job there. Three weeks after my Dad started work we were offered a council house. Mum took Geoff and I up to Harlow to take a look at the house. We'd never been there before. It was just a half hour train journey from where we lived in London.

Harlow was one of 32 new towns built after the war. The government wanted to provide modern housing and factories outside the big cities.

Harlow station now, as shown in the picture above, is very different from the Harlow station of the 1950s. Steam trains were used throughout Britain until the mid-1950s.

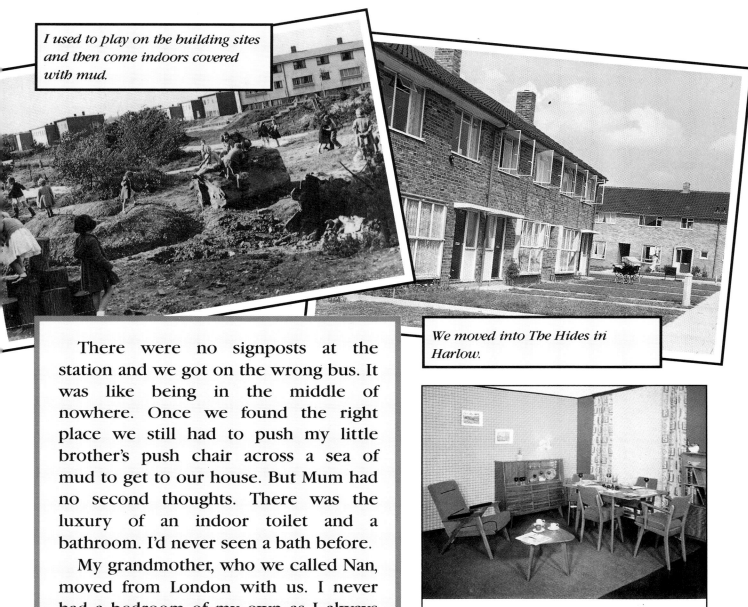

I used to play on the building sites and then come indoors covered with mud.

We moved into The Hides in Harlow.

There were no signposts at the station and we got on the wrong bus. It was like being in the middle of nowhere. Once we found the right place we still had to push my little brother's push chair across a sea of mud to get to our house. But Mum had no second thoughts. There was the luxury of an indoor toilet and a bathroom. I'd never seen a bath before.

My grandmother, who we called Nan, moved from London with us. I never had a bedroom of my own as I always had to share with her.

When we moved to Harlow the house looked quite sparse. We didn't have much furniture except for a few things of my nan's which helped to see us through. She had a few old bits of furniture and a piano which we weren't allowed to touch. I remember going with Mum to buy our first three-piece suite. It was grey and red with vinyl arms – quite the latest thing!

Furniture of Distinction

A family party in our house soon after we arrived in Harlow.

9

Harlow in 1953 was very small. There was the old town which was really just a village and then a few new houses around the edge. Once I had my bike I'd go off for the whole day with a few sandwiches and my butterfly net. I collected lots of things as long as they didn't cost me anything. Stamps were the "in thing" and we all collected cigarette cards and swapped them at school.

Very few people could afford a car when we first lived in Harlow. Dad always walked to work and Mum bought a bike when she got a job. My aunt's family had a car and they used to come up to us for the holidays. Since we had a house and they lived in a flat in London it was mostly that way round. We went blackberrying in the lanes around Harlow and then came back and made pies. It was a treat for them to get into the country.

Harlow was planned with a complete system of cycle tracks to separate cyclists from motor vehicles.

There were so many couples having their first children in Harlow that the town was nicknamed "pramtown".

Isn't Mum clever!

Mum had an office job in Harlow, so my nan looked after us in the school holidays. She did most of the cooking as well. She was always there at lunchtimes when we came home from primary school. Lunch was our one good meal of the day. There was never much for tea, usually bread and dripping or fish paste and home-made cakes to fill us up. Saturday tea was a bit special. We would have fish fingers and tinned tomatoes which were quite a luxury.

My nan did a lot of the cleaning. The only carpet we had was a narrow strip up the stairs with painted wood either side. We had shiny lino on the floor otherwise, so we didn't need a vacuum cleaner. Nan got down on her hands and knees with a stiff brush to clean the stairs.

We had a washing machine with a wringer that slotted in at the back.

The neighbouring children and me outside our house. My red bike was a treasured possession.

The new houses in Harlow were fitted out with mass-produced kitchens.

We had quite a strict routine at home. Friday night was bath night and hair-washing night. We were called in early from the streets on that evening. I think this was a habit that followed on from London where we didn't have a bathroom. There the copper, which was a large copper tub set in brickwork, was lit every Friday night so we could all have hot water for a bath. It was too expensive to heat it up every day.

In Harlow we had a back boiler on the fireplace, so even in the hottest summer the fire had to be lit to provide hot water. We had an electric cooker and no fridge to begin with. We were really excited when we got a fridge. We made our own ice lollies from orange juice.

A typical bathroom in Harlow in the 1950s. In 1951, 37% of households still had no fixed bath.

Television

Bedtime was strictly at eight o'clock sharp. I certainly wasn't allowed to stay up to watch any grown-up programmes on television. My parents watched it a lot as they couldn't afford to go out much when I was young. I used to sneak down the stairs sometimes to peep at the telly through the glass panels in the lounge door. I leapt upstairs again if I heard a chair creak. One programme all the kids wanted to see was *Quatermass and the Pit*. It frightened the life out of me but I still had to watch it.

Six Five Special on a Saturday night was a must. None of my friends would miss it either. It was on this programme that I first saw a lot of my favourite pop singers. We listened to the radio quite a bit but there wasn't much pop music on the radio then.

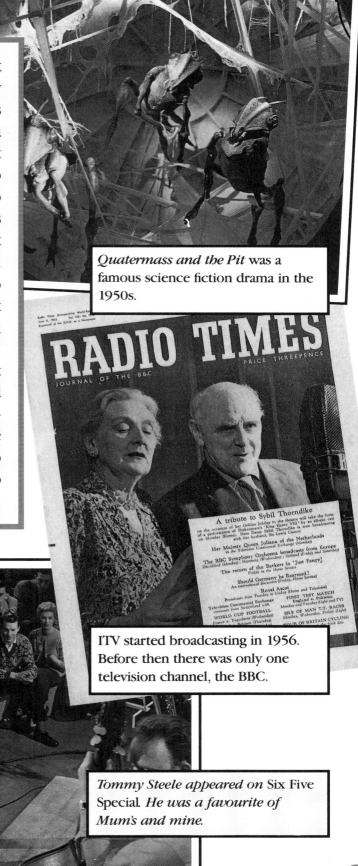

Quatermass and the Pit was a famous science fiction drama in the 1950s.

ITV started broadcasting in 1956. Before then there was only one television channel, the BBC.

Tommy Steele appeared on Six Five Special. *He was a favourite of Mum's and mine.*

13

School days

My first school in Harlow was quite a change after London. It was single storey and much more open. The furniture and everything seemed very modern. I much preferred it even though I didn't know anybody there to begin with.

I was in the Brownies and we were the guard of honour for the royal visit to the local church. It was a big day. We spent ages getting ready beforehand, cleaning shoes and polishing badges. We were there for hours before they arrived. It was worth it though. I shook hands with the Duke of Edinburgh. He was very kind and said he hoped we hadn't got too cold. The Queen walked past us all with her nose in the air!

Harlow Council was proud of the town's development and invited many VIPs and royalty to visit.

We had free school milk every day. It was always warm and tasted a bit off. I pretended to drink mine and then poured it down the sink.

The Brownies' tea party. I'm third along on the left. I never had a party dress.

Me in my first school outfit.

Mark Hall School is now a comprehensive. Technical modern and secondary modern schools mostly became comprehensives after 1973.

I always wore a uniform but it was expensive. Luckily by the time I was twelve I'd learnt to make all my school dresses myself. One of the first things I had to do was make my own netball skirt in the needlework class. Then, every night before games, I ironed the pleats one by one. I used to roll the skirt up and put it in a stocking to keep the pleats in. There were no crease-resistant fabrics then.

When I was young Mum made me wear a liberty bodice. She said I had to be well wrapped up in winter in case I caught a cold. I was so embarrassed I took it off in the toilets as soon as I got to school. I didn't want to be seen in it when we changed for games.

We had cookery lessons and learnt a lot about health and hygiene. People were always worried about getting an infection. We were told to wash any fruit we ate in case we caught a terrible illness called polio. At home I had regular doses of cod liver oil and malt extract to keep me healthy.

Before the 1950s, children were at risk of catching polio, a disabling disease. This risk has been greatly reduced by childhood innoculation.

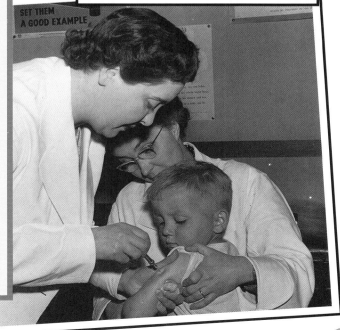

Every morning school started with us being tested on our spellings and our tables. Then there was a general knowledge test. Mark Hall was a technical modern so it was considered inferior to the grammar school. You only went to the grammar school if you'd passed the 11-plus exam. Most of the teachers were men as women only taught cookery, needlework, P.E. and French. Boys did woodwork and metalwork, girls did needlework and cooking. For P.E. and games boys and girls were strictly separate. Even if the hockey pitch touched the soccer pitch we weren't allowed to say "hello" to the boys.

Sport was a very big part of school life. I was quite good at athletics and rounders. My friend Ann and I were always about equal. Sometimes I came first, sometimes she did.

ESSEX · EDUCATION · COMMITTEE

THIS IS TO CERTIFY
that _Pat Howe_
attending the _Mark Hall_
Technical Modern School
has passed the test required for the

PRELIMINARY
SWIMMING
CERTIFICATE
particulars of which are
given on the back hereof.
S.L. Lidefield

Countersigned on behalf of the Committee:
E. E. Hardy Chairman
B. E. Lawrence Chief Education Officer
6th December 1960

I took this photo of my class in the science lab. The teacher didn't seem to mind the cartoon we'd done of him.

It was an exciting day when Roger Bannister broke the record by running a mile in under four minutes.

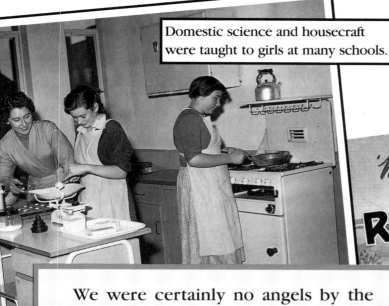

Domestic science and housecraft were taught to girls at many schools.

Harlow was a safe town to cycle in because of all the specially-built cycle tracks. So lots of pupils cycled to school.

'Magic Carpet'
CYCLING WITH
RALEIGH
THE ALL-STEEL BICYCLE
DURING 1958

THE RALEIGH
NOTTINGHAM ENGLAND

We were certainly no angels by the time we reached Mark Hall. On the last day of term we used to stuff newspaper up the exhaust pipe of the teachers' cars. Not many of them had cars but the physics teacher had a Ford Popular. We used to stand at the bus stop and hope he'd give us a lift.

The punishment for bad behaviour at school was being kept in and made to write lines, or sometimes you got a sharp rap on the knuckles with a ruler. One of the boys in my class was slippered by the religious education teacher for making a mess on the floor with chalk during a wet breaktime. If we got into trouble at school we never told our parents.

We spent ages practising with our hula-hoops, during break-times and when we got home. The idea was to keep them going for as long as possible. You had to wiggle your hips very fast to keep the hoop from falling down. I wasn't bad at that. Ann wasn't so good because she never had much of a waist.

The craze for hula-hoops started in the United States, like many other popular trends in the 1950s.

Weekends

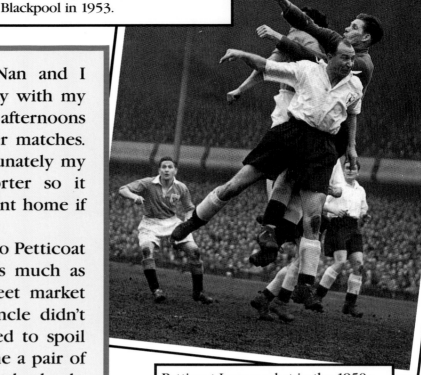

Quite often at weekends Nan and I went back to London to stay with my uncle and aunt. On Saturday afternoons my uncle took me to soccer matches. He was a Spurs man. Unfortunately my dad was an Arsenal supporter so it could be difficult when I went home if Spurs had won.

Sunday mornings we'd go to Petticoat Lane market, just to look as much as anything. A visit to the street market was a bit of a ritual. My uncle didn't have any children so he used to spoil me sometimes. He bought me a pair of mules once, shoes with little heels. Mum disapproved, and said they were unsuitable for me. I still managed to wear them though. Normally the rule of the house was that since Mum was buying my clothes she also chose them.

Petticoat Lane market in the 1950s. Street markets in London's East End are still thriving today.

Most sweets were sold by weight in the 1950s. A wrapped bar was a luxury for most people.

I was always given a comic annual by my uncle and aunt but I bought myself The Dandy.

My parents sent me off to Sunday school despite great objections from me. Since they never went to church I didn't see why I should go to Sunday school. They stayed at home and read the papers. I had a "Sunday best" outfit and a Sunday coat which I wasn't allowed to wear any other day.

Sunday was treat day and we were given money to go to the paper shop and buy a few sweets and some comics. I didn't have regular pocket money. I don't think there was enough money to go round at the end of the week at home. I bought sweets loose in quarter pounds from glass jars. Sometimes I'd stretch to a bar of fruit and nut chocolate. Most of the time wrapped bars seemed too expensive.

There was always a roast dinner without fail on Sundays, followed by apple pie. It was definitely the big meal of the week and we weren't allowed to miss it. For Sunday tea we often had cockles and whelks. They were brought round by a man in a van.

Holidays and celebrations

We always had our summer holiday in Great Yarmouth. From the year I was born 'till when I was fourteen, we only missed out on it the year that we moved to Harlow. We always stayed for two weeks in the same guest house with the same landlady. We spent the whole day on the beach along by the jetty, always at the same spot.

In the evenings we went for a stroll and then to a pub. Geoff and I were left outside on the porch being fed crisps and lemonade. If we wanted something we had to push the door open just enough to stick a hand through and wave. We never went inside the pub.

Sometimes some of our relatives came down from London. They were a bit better off than us so they stayed in a hotel. When they came I was given pineapple juice instead of lemonade.

Mother, grandmother, father and I in Great Yarmouth before Geoff was born.

Paddling was as far as we went. We weren't allowed to swim.

Geoff and I on holiday. We never had any special holiday clothes apart from a swimsuit.

Gorleston-on-Sea is just along the coast from Great Yarmouth.

We flew to Jersey in a four-engined Viscount. I was absolutely terrified.

Jersey Welcomes you

When I was fourteen we went to Jersey. It was the first time I'd been out of England. Dad hired a car to take us to the airport. That felt ever so posh. I had a brand new blue suit and my first pair of high-heeled shoes. They were white and they crippled me but I wasn't going to confess. I felt so grown-up.

I could never have a proper birthday party. Mum just couldn't afford to feed lots of other children. I used to visit one friend who did have parties. Her father was a pilot at Stansted airport. Theirs was a different way of life. They were the only people I knew then who had a telephone.

I was a bridesmaid at several family weddings. When my aunt got married it was a very posh "do". The reception afterwards was in a hotel in London. It was my first time in a hotel. We'd only ever stayed in a guest house when we went on holiday.

I'm the bridesmaid standing in front of the groom. My brother wore his school cap to look smart.

Entertainment

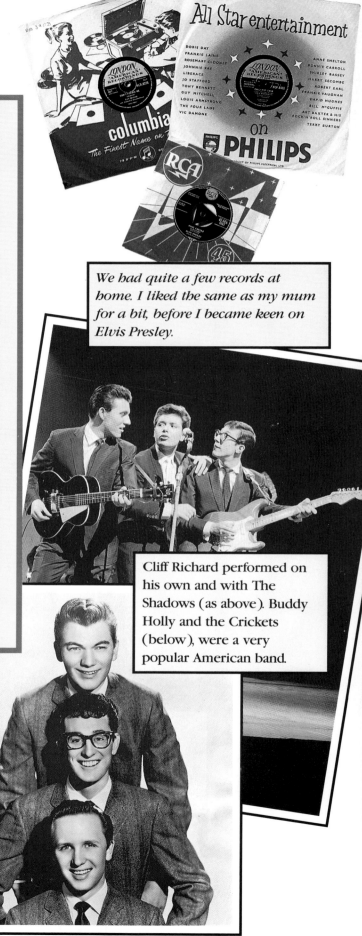

I went round a lot to my friend Ann's house. She had a wind-up gramophone which we played in the garden. We listened to her records. Buddy Holly was her favourite. One of her other girlfriends sat on her pile of 78s. One of them cracked which broke Ann's heart.

I was really into Elvis. He was my heart-throb and I collected all of his albums. Mum and Dad thought he was terrible, and a dangerous influence, so they switched off the television if he was on. I also really liked Cliff Richard. Elvis and Cliff were my two all-time favourites.

Once we were about twelve we went to youth clubs in Harlow. We played table tennis and darts and started to meet boys. Sometimes we went to dances and spent ages beforehand practising jiving at home. We felt very daring when our skirts flew up above our knees.

We had quite a few records at home. I liked the same as my mum for a bit, before I became keen on Elvis Presley.

Cliff Richard performed on his own and with The Shadows (as above). Buddy Holly and the Crickets (below), were a very popular American band.

I went with Mum to buy a radiogram from a shop on the High. It was a great big polished wooden thing on legs with a heavy lid. Mum couldn't afford to pay for it all at once so she bought it on the H.P. which we called the "never never". She used hire purchase or H.P. for big items but only ever for one thing at a time. She wanted to be sure she could keep up the repayments. Mum always worked out her money very carefully.

Mostly we went shopping at the Stow shopping centre. I often went down there on my bike or my roller skates to run errands for my mum.

The Stow shopping centre today and in 1953. There were still bread shortages then.

Spending-money

I did a daily paper round for years. I earned five bob a week, or seven-and-six if there were no complaints. Sometimes I put the wrong paper through the wrong door. If that happened then I lost money. I used to hate the people who took the *Times* as it was so heavy. Most people took *The Herald*.

As soon as I was old enough I worked on Saturday and Sunday mornings in a little sweet shop. I earned two bob an hour there. I treated myself to a hairdo and still felt quite wealthy at the end of it.

Once I had my own money I could do what I wanted with it. When it came to buying clothes I always wanted what was fashionable but Mum always wanted to get me something serviceable. Mum and Dad didn't have a lot of money floating around. If I wanted something I had to go and earn it.

Dresses with bold prints and full skirts were the thing.

Persil for Coloureds, too!

In the 1950s, for the first time teenagers had the money to choose their own fashions and hairstyles.

The fashion for girls and women to wear trousers, which had become common during the war, really took off during the 1950s.

REGAL CINEMA
HARLOW
Phone 24089

SUNDAY 27 JANUARY
Doors open: 4.0 p.m.

Humphrey Bogart, June Allyson
BATTLE CIRCUS
(A) — 5.45, 8.35

Hugh McDermott, Elspeth Gray, JOHNNY ON THE SPOT (U) 4.30, 7.15

MONDAY, 28 JANUARY
Doors open:
Mon., Tues. 3.55; Wed. 1.20 p.m.
WE PROUDLY ANNOUNCE
THE RETURN OF
JACK HAWKINS
DONALD SINDEN
DENHOLM ELLIOTT
VIRGINIA McKENNA
in
THE CRUEL SEA
(U) — Mon., Tues. 5.05, 8.25
Wed. 1.50, 5.05, 8.25

Bob Monkhouse
ALL IN GOOD FUN
(U) — Mon., Tues. Wed. 3.55, 7.15

THURSDAY, 31 JANUARY
Doors open:
Thurs., Fri. 5.0; Sat. 1.50 p.m.
SPENCER TRACY
ROBERT WAGNER
co-starring CLAIRE TREVOR
THE MOUNTAIN
(U) — Colour by Technicolor
VistaVision
Thurs., Fri. 5.30, 8.40
Sat. 2.20, 5.30, 8.40

Leo Gorcey, Huntz Hall
and the Bowery Boys
DIG THAT URANIUM
(U) — Thurs., Fri. 7.15
Sat. 4.05, 7.15

The Regal Cinema, Harlow, in the 1950s.

My nan took me to see several Norman Wisdom films.

The only thing I spent much money on was the Saturday morning pictures. I didn't have pocket money as such, just sixpence for the pictures and some pennies for an ice cream in the interval. If you were a regular you were given a special arm band to wear and then you could sit in the back row.

There was always a cartoon, a serial and a western. The whole morning the cinema was full of boos and cheers. You always went back next week for the next episode of the serial. The manager ran a children's talent competition in the interval. I never went in for that.

Later on I'd go with a friend to try and get into an adult certificate film. We put on quite a bit of lipstick to make ourselves look older. Then we waited outside for a friendly looking adult. We gave them our money and asked them to buy tickets for us.

ELVIS
2 IN HIS BIGGEST SINGING SWINGING HITS!

M-G-M presents
ELVIS PRESLEY in
"JAIL-HOUSE ROCK"
With JUDY TYLER DEAN JONES
Directed by Richard Thorpe

M-G-M Presents
ELVIS PRESLEY in
"It Happened at the World's Fair"
With JOAN O'BRIEN · GARY LOCKWOOD

Leaving school

I wanted to become a teacher so I stayed on at school after 'O' levels. My parents weren't that keen on education but they did support me once I'd decided what I wanted to do. A lot of my friends left school at fifteen. I was a bit envious of them going out and earning money straight away. but I reckoned it was worth staying on. Girls didn't often do maths or science then but I did two maths 'A' levels and geography before going on to teacher training college.

I teach maths now in a comprehensive school in Harlow, near to where I live. My husband Les was born in one of the old parts of Harlow and we live with our two children in the area where he was brought up.

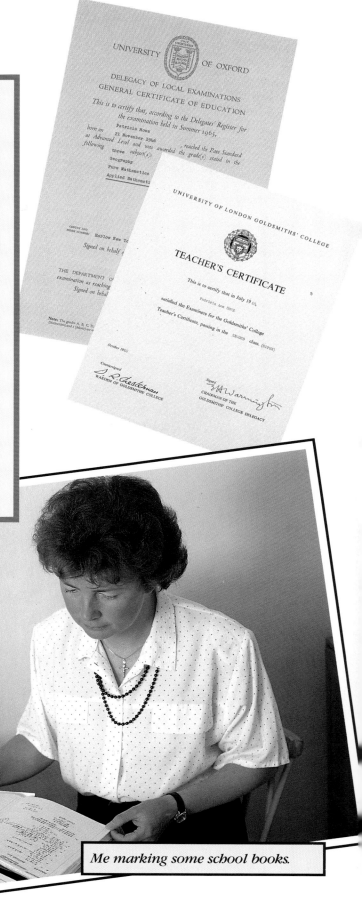

Me marking some school books.

In the news

These are some of the important events which happened during Pat's childhood.

1950 British troops were sent to South Korea after the communist invasion from North Korea was condemned by the United Nations Security Council.

1951 The Festival of Britain was held on the south bank of the Thames in London to celebrate post-war progress. The Royal Festival Hall remained afterwards as a modern concert hall.

1952 King George VI of Britain died while his daughter, Princess Elizabeth, was on safari in Kenya.

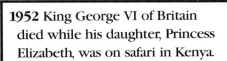

1953 Mount Everest was climbed by Hillary and Tensing. They used oxygen supplies on the last stage of their climb up the world's highest mountain.

1954 France sent 20,000 troops to the French colony of Algeria as the war of independence began.

1955 Sir Winston Churchill, aged eighty-one, resigned as prime minister. He was succeeded by Sir Anthony Eden.

1956 Colonel Nasser, the President of Egypt, took control of the Suez Canal. Britain and France sent troops to regain control of the shipping route but were forced to back down.

1957 The USSR launched Sputnik I, the first satellite to orbit the Earth.

1958 The Campaign for Nuclear Disarmament was formed. Several thousand people marched to Aldermaston to protest against the development of nuclear weapons there.

1959 In Cuba, General Batista's dictatorship was defeated by the popular uprising led by Fidel Castro.

Things to do

Many of your relatives or neighbours will have memories of the 1950s. Show them this book and ask them how their lives in the 1950s compared with Pat Scott's. Ask them what they remember of big events, such as the Queen's coronation.

If you have a cassette-recorder you could tape their memories. Before you visit people make a list of the things you want to talk about. Ask them about where they lived in the early 1950s and whether their home was very different by the end of the decade.

THREE PIECE SUITE

only
21 GNS.

Find out when the house or flat that you live in now was built. If you live in an area that was rebuilt after the war see if you can find out what it was like before. Your local library might have photos of the streets as they used to be.

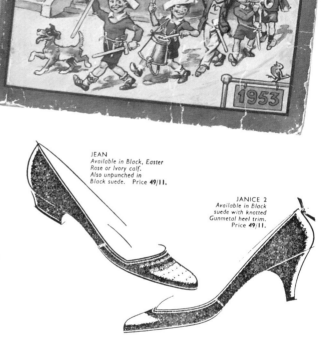

JEAN
Available in Black, Easter Rose or Ivory calf. Also unpunched in Black suede. Price 49/11.

JANICE 2
Available in Black suede with knotted Gunmetal heel trim. Price 49/11.

Some people may still have photos of the period, as well as magazines, newspapers or records. Ask if you can look at them. If you do get hold of some 1950's records, either by borrowing them from the library or from friends, see if you can learn to jive.

Go to your local library. Ask to see any newspapers from the 1950s. Your local museum may have a collection of furniture or objects from the period.

Index

Series design: David Bennett
Design: Sally Boothroyd
Editor/picture researcher: Sarah Ridley

Acknowledgements: the author and publisher would like to thank Pat Scott, Jackie Storey, David Devine and the Harlow Study Centre for their help in the preparation of this book.

Photographs: Associated Press 17b, 28b; BBC 13t; British Film Institute Stills, Posters and Designs 25b; Mary Evans/Bruce Castle Museum 4b; John Frost Historical Newspaper Service endpapers, 7; Harlow Study and Visitors Centre 8t, 8b, 9tl, 9tr, 10c, 10b, 12tl, 12b, 14t, 14br, 23b, 25t, 30cr, 30b; Harlow Council/Eastern Daily Times 15tr; Hulton-Deutsch Collection 17tl, 19tl, 21tl, 24bl; Jersey Museums Service 21tr; Kobal Collection cover tl, 25c; Norfolk Museums Service 20br; Robert Opie Collection 5b, 7bl, 7br, 19tr, 22bl, 24t, 30t, 31b; Popperfoto cover bl, 6b, 13b, 15b, 16br, 18t, 22c, 24br, 27(all), 28tr, 29tl, 29c, 29b; Royal Geographical Society 28tl; Neil Thomson 8c, 15tl, 23c, 26b; Topham 18b, 22br, 29tr.

A CIP Catalogue record for this book is available from the British Library.

Printed in Great Britain by Cambus Litho.